Flourishing Finances Workbook

Gerlisa D. Shipman

TTL Publishing

WAKE FOREST, NORTH CAROLINA

Flourishing Finances Workbook by Gerlisa D. Shipman
TTL Publishing
Wake Forest, North Carolina 27588
info@tokunbotheleader.com
Visit the publisher's website at tokunbotheleader.com.

Visit the author's website at bloomanista.org.

Cover Design by Adriane Racquel Creative.

Unless otherwise noted, all scriptures are taken from the New International Version Bible.

Flourishing Finances Workbook /**Gerlisa D. Shipman**
ISBN: 978-1-958347-03-4

This Workbook Belongs to

Given to Me By

Started on

Contents

Letter from the Author

Dear Bloomanista,

You are on a journey of developing into everything that God has created you to be. As you secure your identity in Christ, you will discover your purpose in God. While you are on a journey of understanding your purpose, you will need to learn strategies that will help you get to the very place God has ordained for you to be. As your favorite bloomanista, my mission is to show you the steps to secure your identity, activate your purpose, become generous, get to the root cause of bad spending, pray effectively, and create a budget. This workbook works closely with the main textbook, Flourishing Finances: Teaching Bloomanistas Financial Responsibility. The book will also help you to dive deeper into the subjects listed above.

Through this workbook, you will be guided in learning how to have a godly perspective on your finances, and you will be taught how to fully rely on God with your money. The foundational practices taught in this workbook about money will help you create a system to help you move fully towards your purpose. When it is time to walk in the fullness of your purpose, you will know how to manage your money well and reach your God-given goals. I'm so excited about your journey!!

Love,

Gerlisa D. Shipman

"Your Favorite Bloomanista"

Words to Know

The following are words to be familiar with as you work through this guide.

Identity- A secure, confident knowing of who you are, where you came from, why you are here, and who you belong to. Through your Lord and Savior Jesus Christ, you have power and access to anything that you need. When you are secure in your identity, your only concern is to please the One who made you.

Purpose- The thing that you were created to do on earth. It is a problem that you were born to solve. All of your God-given talents and natural abilities are attached to a problem that God wants to solve on earth.

Tithing- A sacrificial offering that is introduced in the Old Testament and still practiced by New Testament Believers. We give God 10 percent of our monetary increase plus more.

Generosity- A form of giving of your time, talents, and treasure (money) that is cheerful, altruistic, and kind.

Retail Therapy- Shopping to alleviate emotional discomfort.

Budget- A strategic plan on how to manage your finances to meet a need or goal.

Faith- Believing God for something that He has promised you even though you cannot see it.

Miracles- A seemingly impossible moment, task, and idea that God makes possible.

Bloomanista-A teenager or young adult female that is dedicated to becoming a better version of herself. She is committed to learning and growing so that she can be all that God created her to be.

Affirmations- An encouraging, hopeful, or clear proclamation that is declared over oneself or to another human.

One

Understanding that You Are God-Given

Part 1: Understanding Identity – It's God-Given

Directions: Take some time to reflect on the following questions. Refer back to the definition of identity to help you with these questions.

Identity- A secure, confident knowing of who you are, where you came from, why you are here, and who you belong to. Through your Lord and Savior Jesus Christ, you have power and access to anything that you need. When you are secure in your identity, your only concern is to please the One who made you.

1. In what areas of your life do you think you need to secure your identity?

___

___

___

2. How do you know that your identity is fully secure in Christ?

____

____

____

3. What are some ways that you can remind yourself daily of who you are in Christ?

____

____

____

Identity Affirmations Activity

Directions: Take out your phone and put the camera on yourself. Switch the setting to video and press the start or record button. Hold this book upward, but not blocking your face so that you can read the following affirmations to yourself. If you do not have a phone, you can use a mirror or something that shows your reflection. Read one of the affirmations confidently while looking at the camera.

1. Christ died on the cross for me; therefore, I lack nothing!

2. I am fully known, seen, heard, loved, forgiven, and worth it.

3. God made me a masterpiece when He created me in my mother's womb.

4. I am never abandoned, forgotten, or condemned. God really loves me.

5. My Father in Heaven is the King of Kings, and I'm His royal creation.

6. Girl everything about you is unique, valuable, and priceless.

7. Everything I need is in Jesus Christ. His opinion about me is the only opinion that matters. I am secure in Christ, and I lack nothing.

Part 2: Your Talents - It's God-Given

Directions: Answer the reflection questions below based on the definition of talent.

Talent- A natural ability that you have that takes little effort to do.

1. List things that you are naturally good at.

    1. ______________________________

    2. ______________________________

    3. ______________________________

4. ______________________________

5. ______________________________

6. ______________________________

2. List 3 talents that you need to focus on right now?

1. ______________________________

2. ______________________________

3. ______________________________

3. How will you dedicate your talents back to God?

____

____

____

____

____

____

____

____

____

Part 3: Your Purpose is God-Given

Directions: Take some time to reflect on the following questions while referring back to the definition of purpose.

Purpose- The thing that you were created to do on earth. All of your God-given talents and natural abilities are attached to a problem that God wants to solve on earth.

1. Have you asked God what your purpose is? If so, what has God shown you?

____

____

____

Activate Your Purpose: 5 Steps to Finding Your Purpose

Open Your Heart	Before you invite God to do anything in your life, you must fully open yourself up to receive whatever He has to say. You have to let go of your expectations and preconceived notions of what you think your life will look like and prepare your heart to hear whatever He may say. Consistent worship will help you remember who God is, and it will open your heart to Him. Create a heart posture that's inviting.
Prayer and Fasting	Go to God and simply ask Him what your purpose is. Ask Him what you are called to do, where are you going, and why you are here on earth. The more you pray these prayers, the more God will show you the answers. He may speak through prophets (messengers from God), His Word (Bible), sermons, friends, dreams, and children. Those are a few examples, but I wouldn't limit the ways God can speak to you. Times of concentration through fasting will help you hear clearly. The more you spend time with God and allow Him to secure your identity, the more He will prepare you and show you your purpose. Become desperate to know what God wants to do with you.

Trust The Process	You may not get all of your answers in one day, but trust that God has given you the right path and is leading you. Take one step at a time in obedience and trust the process. Soon you will find that all the pieces will connect. What you think might be meaningless, still has a purpose.
Reflect Often	Journaling will be a key part of understanding your purpose. It's important to document dreams, prophetic words, experiences, and thoughts. Some things you may not understand now, but you will understand in the future. Everything will come full circle so I encourage you to journal your process. Ask questions about what you feel, why you feel that way, and what it means.
Follow The Holy Spirit	There will be times the Holy Spirit prompts or asks you to do something without you fully understanding why. If you feel peace and confidence about what He has shown you, no matter how crazy it seems to other people, MOVE! God will show you everything that you need when you make that first step. After you confess with your mouth that Jesus is Lord and believe in your heart that God has raised Him from the dead, you will be saved (Romans 10:9-10). You receive authority once you are saved, but you receive power to follow God once you are filled by the Holy Ghost. You can be filled by the Holy Ghost by asking God to baptize you or fill you with the Holy Ghost. Through the baptism in the Holy Ghost, God gives you the gift of speaking in tongues. (1 Corinthians 14:2). I encourage you to pray about being baptized in the Holy Spirit.

Directions:
Step 1: Write your name in the first bigger circle below.
Step 2: Fill in the attribute web (the eight smaller circles) by answering these questions below.

What are recurring or repeated events, ideas, passions, or desires that you have?
What breaks your heart? (Example: Seeing people homeless)

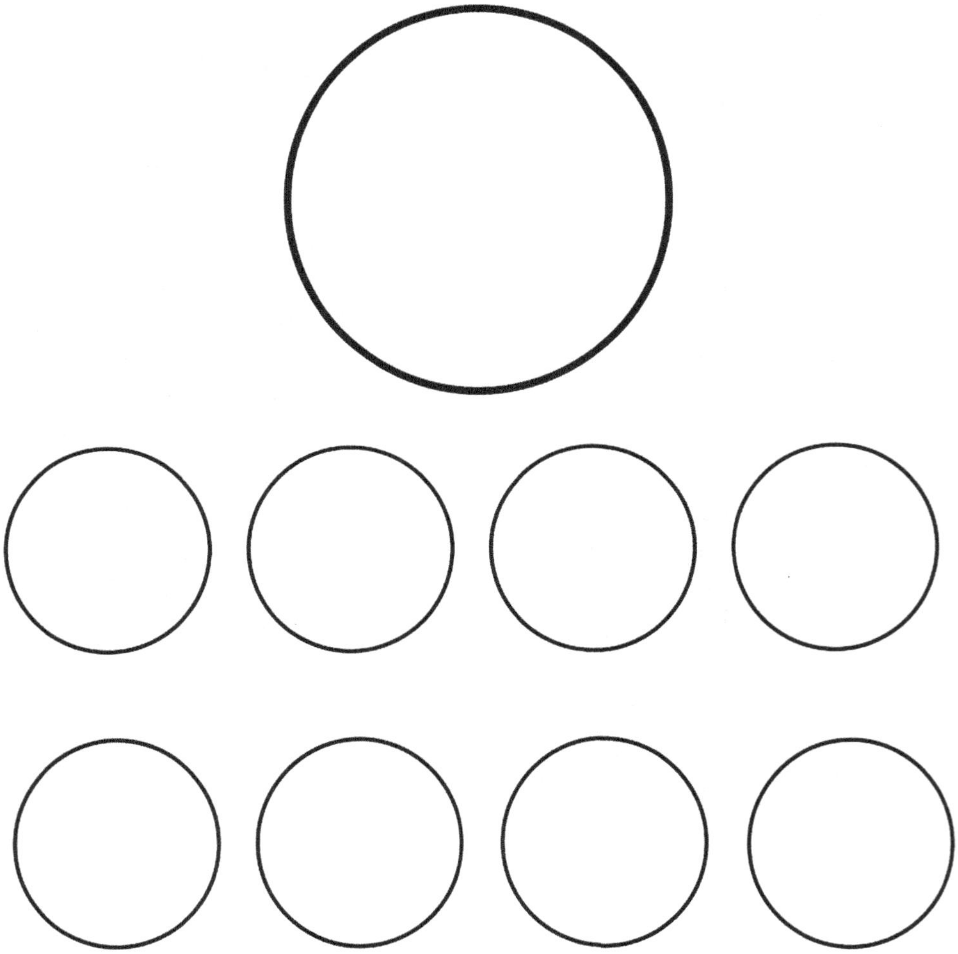

Part 4: God-Given Dreams and Goals

Directions: Answer the following reflection questions below.

1. Think back to when you were a child. What did you say you wanted to be when you grew up? Ask your parents or God to help you remember.

____

____

____

____

2. Using the box below, draw a picture of a dream or desire you have. (Example: A bloomanista who desires to open a coffee shop to provide jobs for ex-cons will draw a picture of a coffee shop.)

Two

Blossoming into a Giver

Part 1: Tithing Principle

Directions: Complete this self-reflection on tithing by using the following questions and definition of tithing below.

<u>Tithing-</u> A sacrificial offering that is mandated in the Old Testament. We give God a minimum of 10 percent of our monetary increase. As New Testament Believers and cheerful givers, we give more than 10 percent as a form of worship to God.

1. If you do not tithe, what has kept you from tithing?

2. What are some ways that you can be consistent in tithing?

____

____

____

____

Part 2: Generosity Reflection

Directions: Take some time to reflect on the following questions while referring back to the definition of generosity.

Generosity- A form of giving that is cheerful, altruistic, and kind. Freely giving to others your time, talent, and treasure (money).

1. What is one of the biggest reasons you hesitate to be generous?

____

____

____

____

2. What are some ways you can be generous with your time, money, and talents?

____

____

____

____

3. What are some things that you believe God is challenging you to do to grow as a giver?

____

____

____

____

4. What are some reasons you fail to be obedient when God challenges you to be a better giver?

____

____

____

____

Part 3: Generosity Challenge

Directions: Put a bookmark on this chapter to help you easily refer back to this chapter. Choose 3 generosity challenges to do over the next two weeks. Put a checkbox by the ones you complete. Repeat this challenge as many times as you feel led to do so.

Before You Start
1. Don’t expect anything in return, including a thank you. 2. Don't let everyone know what you did. (Matthew 6:3-4) 3. Treat this person as if it was Jesus you were serving. (Matthew 25:40) 4. Be cheerful. (2 Corinthians 9:6-7) 5. Use Wisdom. Wisdom is the application of knowledge. Because we do not know everything and we fear(reverence) the Lord, we fully rely on God’s wisdom for our decision-making. We use good judgment before giving. We are not led by our assumptions, emotions, and people-pleasing.

Challenge Yourself

- ☐ Give someone a ride.
- ☐ Pay for the person's meal behind you.
- ☐ Buy something from a friend's or family member's business.
- ☐ Think about a gift or talent that you have. Research an organization that you can volunteer with or look for a way to do this at your church. Volunteer your time, gift, and talent with this organization.
- ☐ Give a little extra in offering on Sunday.
- ☐ Ask God to lay someone on your heart to give money to.
- ☐ Give an affirmation or compliment to a classmate that you normally don't talk to.
- ☐ Share your favorite meal with someone. (I mean the meal you want for yourself.)
- ☐ Help the elderly with a task that is difficult for them to complete.
- ☐ Look for a need in your neighborhood like picking up trash. Give your time and talent to fix this need.
- ☐ Repost/share an event that a person is hosting and needs support.

Three

Deeper Issues of Spending

Part 1: Let's Get To The Root

Direction: Refer to chapter 3 in the Flourishing Finances book to read more about issues that control our spending. Circle the number on the scale that best relates to your deeper issues of spending. Make sure you are being honest with yourself!

1. **Rejection**- A feeling of abandonment and exclusion.						
Doesn't Relate	1	2	3	4	5	I can definitely relate

2. **Attention Seeking**- Actions that are done for approval from others.						
Doesn't Relate	1	2	3	4	5	I can definitely relate

3. **Media Influence**- Decisions made based on things seen on social media.						
Doesn't Relate	1	2	3	4	5	I can definitely relate

4. **Poor Body Image**- Not liking what you see when you look at yourself in the mirror. Being very self-critical.						
Doesn't Relate	1	2	3	4	5	I can definitely relate

5. **Acceptance** - Wanting approval from peers and those around you.						
Doesn't Relate	1	2	3	4	5	I can definitely relate

Part 2: Reflection Questions

Directions: Take some time to reflect on the following questions.

1. Have I ever noticed that when I am feeling down mentally, my spending habits change for better or worse?

____

____

____

____

2. Instead of looking for materialistic ways to solve my issues, how can I give my burdens to God and pursue wholeness?

____

____

____

____

3. When it comes to my finances, how can I practice the fruits of the spirit, especially self-control?

____

____

*** Note: If this is a difficult area for you, remind yourself of who you are! Refer to the cell phone affirmation exercise in Chapter 1 of this workbook.**

Four

A Bloominista's Prayers

Part 1: Aligning Your Prayers with Where God is Taking You!

Directions: Answer the following questions.

1. Do parts of my prayer life involve asking God to meet my financial needs? If not, how can I start communicating to God about what I need financially?

2. In what ways can you prevent fear and doubt from taking over your thought life?

____

____

____

3. What are some things you would like to believe God for in the area of your finances?

____

____

____

____

4. Take a moment to think about how God provided financial miracles for you and your family in the past. Based on that knowledge, how can you believe in Him for more starting today?

____

____

____

____

Part 2: 5-Day Prayer Challenge

Directions: Place a bookmark here so that you can easily refer to these prayers. Say each prayer twice a day or repeat it as many times as needed. This will help you get started on how to talk to God about these topics.

Day 1: Secure My Identity *
God, I thank You for the many ways that You plan to use me in the future to bring out Your will on Earth. As I continue to grow in you, I pray that you secure my identity so that I can fully walk in my purpose. Send me people that will affirm my God-given talents and help push me into my destiny. Help me to not reject the people that you send in my life that will help me bloom. Help me to recognize the divine connections that you are sending me. I pray for a heart to serve you. As my Father in Heaven, help me to look for you in every area of my life and be completely filled up with your love. God, let Your will be done in my life for Your glory. In Jesus' name, I pray Amen!

Day 2: A Generous Heart *
Thank You, God, for giving me breath in my body and air in my lungs. I am thankful that everything was created through You and for You. You are the giver of all things, and I thank You that you are a generous God. I pray that You give me a heart that is generous, cheerful, and obedient in my finances. Give me wisdom on who, what, when, where, and how to give. Help me to not look for praise when I give, but to give with a pure heart. I pray that it may be a sweet sound of worship to You when I offer my finances in this way. I pray that I am constantly reminded of Your miracles and blessings each day. In Jesus' name, I pray Amen!

Day 3: Digging Up The Root *

Dear Heavenly Father, I thank You that You are a God that makes my burdens light. I can find rest in Your sovereignty and be confident that You can be trusted to keep Your promises. I pray that You help me to become a woman that doesn't look for peace and joy outside of You. Help me to not hide behind materialism that masks any insecurities and lies. Reveal every stronghold and help me to look for You to mend my broken pieces. I pray that I will come boldly to the throne of grace and find sweet rest. As You restore any brokenness, let me be reminded of Your goodness, power, and the small victories that You give daily. Give me the strength, wisdom, and power to walk in your spirit. In Jesus' name, I pray Amen!

Day 4: A Prayer of Faith and Provision *

Dear Father, You are Jehovah-Jireh. In Your Word, You told me to cast my cares on You because You care for me. You also said to tell You what I need. I thank You for what You have already done and expect Your peace to surpass all of my limited understanding. Father, I pray that You help my faith to rise as I believe You for the things I can't see. Take away every anxiety and thought that is filled with fear. According to Your Word, You hold all power in Your hands. I pray that You blow my mind with miracles. As You provide, help me to share the testimonies with others. Let my foundation be firm and trust You solely. In Jesus' name, I pray Amen!

Day 5: Honesty About Finances *

Dear God, I pray that You protect my heart from being consumed by the love of money. Help me to be honest with how I receive money. Remind me that You are Lord over everything, and my dependence should solely be on You. Protect me from the wiles and schemes of the enemy concerning my finances. Help me to be patient in making financial decisions and seek discernment. Shut down every operation that is not like You and bring order to my finances. As Your daughter, give me wisdom in this area of my life so that it may bring glory to Your name. In Jesus' name, I pray. Amen!

Five

Creating a Bloomanista's Budget

Part 1: Budgeting Reflection Questions

Directions: Reflect on the following questions. Answer as honestly as possible. Use the definition of budgeting to help you with this section.

<u>Budget-</u> A strategic plan on how to manage your personal finances to meet a need or goal.

1. Do you think budgeting is important? Why or why not?

2. What do you think are the causes of a person who does not budget?

____

____

____

____

3. What do you think are the effects of a person that does or does not budget?

____

____

____

____

Part 2: Budgeting Worksheets

Phase One Budget Worksheet

Directions: The first step in creating a budget is understanding your long-term and short-term goals. Refer to the example below to list all of your long-term and short-term goals in the blank chart provided.

Example

What are your long-term goals? (6 months- 1 year)	In the next 6 months, I want to have: $600 saved towards getting a car $450 saved towards taking a summer trip $400 saved towards my prom dress
What are your short-term goals? (3 months)	In the next 3 months, I want to have half of my long-term goals met: $300 saved towards getting a car $150 saved towards taking a summer trip $200 saved towards my prom dress

What are your long term goals? (6 months-1 year)	What are your short term goals? (3 months)

Phase Two Budget Worksheet

Directions: Using the chart below, list your weekly, biweekly and monthly income.

For example,

I bring home $160 weekly, $320 biweekly, and $640 every month.

Directions: Fill in the blank by answering the statements below.

I make________________________every week.

I make________________________biweekly. (Multiply your weekly income by two.)

I make _______________________every month. (Multiply your biweekly income by two.)

Directions: List your monthly expenses and organize your expenses by importance using the color key.

My Monthly Expenses:
Tithes $64
Offering $20
Phone Bill $72
Bus Fare $60
Car Fund $100
Summer Trip $52
Prom Dress $72
Extra $200 (Entertainment-Hair, nails, movies, mall, etc.)

Directions: Write out in detail what you spend money on every month. Write your total at the top.

Example

Monthly Budget Total $640
Tithes $64 Offering $20 Phone Bill $72 Bus Fare $60 Car Fund $100 Summer Trip $52 Prom Dress $72 Extra $200 (Entertainment-Hair, nails, movies, mall, etc.)

Monthly Budget Total $_______
List below all of the items that you are responsible for each month.

Phase Three Budget Worksheet

Directions: In the next section, you will write out your total for your biweekly budget. Refer to the example below to create your own biweekly budget list. *Using your monthly budget, divide each number by two to create your biweekly budget.

Example

Biweekly Budget Total $360
Tithes $32 Offering $10 Phone Bill $36 Bus Fare $30 Car Fund $50 Summer Trip $26 Prom Dress $36 Extra $100 (Entertainment-Hair, nails, movies, mall, etc.)

Biweekly Budget Total $_______
List below all of the items you are responsible for biweekly.

Directions: Read the example below to determine your weekly budget. *Using your biweekly expenses, divide each number by two to create your weekly budget. Place your answers in the blank chart below.

Example

Weekly Budget Total <u>$160</u>
Tithes $16 Offering $5 Phone Bill $18 Bus Fare $15 Car Fund $25 Summer Trip $13 Prom Dress $18 Extra $50 (Entertainment-Hair, nails, movies, mall, etc.)

Weekly Budget Total $_______
List below all of the items you are responsible for weekly.

*****Optional last step. If you want to see how the entire budget works together, use this chart below to combine your weekly, biweekly, and monthly budgets.**

Example: Your budget should look similar to this when you are finished.

Weekly $160	**Biweekly $360**	**Monthly $640**
Tithes $16 Offering $5 Phone Bill $18 Bus Fare $15 Car Fund $25 Summer Trip $13 Prom Dress $18 Extra $50 (Entertainment-Hair, nails, movies, mall, etc.)	Tithes $32 Offering $10 Phone Bill $36 Bus Fare $30 Car Fund $50 Summer Trip $26 Prom Dress $36 Extra $100 (Entertain-ment-Hair, nails, movies, mall, etc.)	Tithes $64 Offering $20 Phone Bill $72 Bus Fare $60 Car Fund $100 Summer Trip $52 Prom Dress $72 Extra $200 (Entertain-ment-Hair, nails, movies, mall, etc.)

Directions: Use this chart below to map out all of your weekly, biweekly, and monthly expenses. This is your official budget!

Weekly $_______	Biweekly $_______	Monthly $_______

Other Tips on Budgeting

• **Budget Holidays-** If you know Christmas or someone's birthday is coming up and you want to get your family gifts, put them in your budget a couple of months before so you won't be caught off guard.

• **Budgeting Tools-**This is an example of how budgeting will look on paper. Some may find budgeting apps, spreadsheets, and envelopes helpful.

• **Use This Template-** If you have a group that you lead or a business that you have, you can use this same template to budget the finances for those groups or businesses.

• **Be Patient-** It takes time to reach your goals. As long as you discipline yourself and be consistent, you will reach your goals before you know it. You will always be on your way to creating generational wealth and responsibility.

• **Don't Forget Your Little One-** If you have a child, a sibling, or a pet that you take care of, don't forget to include their expenses in your budget.

• **Allow Grace-**You will make mistakes and that's okay. God is the only one that's perfect. Your job is to learn from your mistakes and get back up to try again.

• **Be Positive-** Watch what you say and think! Death and life are in the power of your tongue and you shall eat the fruit thereof. Money may look a little funny at times, but remember how you speak about your money. Even on your worst days, what you say can determine what happens in the future. Having a growth mindset and saying things like, "I had a bad week with not sticking to my budget but I am learning, growing and I will get better."

• **Repeat-** Revisit your budget every three months or as often as you need to check your progress or to make adjustments due to life changes.

• **Give Each Dollar An Assignment -** Every dollar in your budget should have an assignment. If your money doesn't have an assignment, you could easily get into the habit of just spending.

Encouraging Note

Dear Bloomanista,

Congratulations on taking one of the most crucial steps of your life. Understanding financial responsibility is going to be one of the many things that God uses to push you into your destiny. Although you may make mistakes along the way, I believe God will always use these things that seem like setbacks to teach you and grow you. My prayer is that you are like a tree planted along a riverbank, with roots that reach deep into the water. Such trees are not bothered by the heat or worried by long months of drought. Their leaves stay green, and they never stop producing fruit. (See Jeremiah 17:8).

Love,

Gerlisa D. Shipman

"Your Favorite Bloomanista"

Efflorescence Girls, LLC
Grooming Her To Bloom

Know the Author

Gerlisa D. Shipman

Gerlisa D. Shipman is a Metro Atlanta native whose life mission is to serve through leadership. She graduated from Chowan University with a degree in psychology/counseling. Throughout her college career, she started the university's first online publication, she was a student-athlete and she was the first black female Student Government Association president amongst other things.

After graduating in 2015, Gerlisa moved to Chicago where she found a deep love for social justice. She worked for several nonprofit organizations building a volunteer program, organizing around education policy, and working with youth networks on the westside of Chicago.

In 2020, Gerlisa accepted the call to come back home to Georgia and pursue teaching and entrepreneurship. She is currently an elementary school teacher in Metro Atlanta and the CEO and Founder of Efflorescence Girls, LLC. Efflorescence Girls, LLC is a faith-based organization designed to mentor teenage girls and young adult women to have a Godly perspective on identity, relationships, mental health, self-love, life goals, and financial literacy. Gerlisa plans to continue to innovate through servant leadership in various capacities and live out her mantra which is, "Go Be Great!"

Stay Connected with Gerlisa D. Shipman

Efflorescence Girls, LLC

@bloomanista

@bloomanista

bloomanista.org

info@efflorescencegirlsllc.com

TTL Publishing

tokunbotheleader.com

Made in the USA
Coppell, TX
05 November 2026

11302309R00026